Memories of Memphis

A History in Postcards

MEMPHIS, TENN. Confederate Monument. Elmwood Park.

Schiffer Publishing Ltd

Ginny Parfitt with
Mary L. Martin

4880 Lower Valley Road, Atglen, PA 19310 USA

Acknowledgments

Thank you to Steve and Dean McFarland, life-long residents of Memphis, who graciously allowed me to photograph their extensive collection of Memphis postcards and memorabilia, many of which are used in this book. In addition to ephemera, they also have a wonderful collection of Confederate Veterans Reunion memorabilia. As well, some of helmets shown in *Head Dress of Imperial Germany 1880-1916,* published by the Schiffer Military Division, were previously owned by Mr. McFarland.

Published by Schiffer Publishing Ltd.
4880 Lower Valley Road
Atglen, PA 19310
Phone: (610) 593-1777; Fax: (610) 593-2002
E-mail: Info@schifferbooks.com

Copyright © 2005 by Ginny Parfitt with Mary L. Martin
Library of Congress Control Number: 2005924220

Designed by Mark David Bowyer
Type set in PhyllisD/Zurich Lt BT

ISBN: 0-7643-2288-5
Printed in China

For the largest selection of fine reference books on this and related subjects, please visit our web site at **www.schifferbooks.com**
We are always looking for people to write books on new and related subjects. If you have an idea for a book please contact us at the above address.

This book may be purchased from the publisher.
Include $3.95 for shipping.
Please try your bookstore first.
You may write for a free catalog.

In Europe, Schiffer books are distributed by
Bushwood Books
6 Marksbury Ave.
Kew Gardens
Surrey TW9 4JF England
Phone: 44 (0) 20 8392-8585; Fax: 44 (0) 20 8392-9876
E-mail: info@bushwoodbooks.co.uk
Free postage in the U.K., Europe; air mail at cost.

Contents

58

History

High above the mighty Mississippi River, far enough away and high enough to be clear of periodic river flooding, the city of Memphis took hold. Its founding fathers, James Winchester, John Overton, and Andrew "Old Hickory" Jackson, evidently put much thought and planning into its location. They must have felt that the safety provided by the Chickasaw bluff, one of four in that geographic location, provided a certain amount of natural security; years earlier, the bluffs had been used as a fort for early explorers, both French and Spanish. An inspection of the surrounding countryside found it to be relatively flat and fertile, with enough yearly precipitation to support a substantial agricultural economy. Most importantly, Memphis was located about midway between the Ohio Valley to the north and New Orleans to the south – a strategic location for a river port and trading center. The city charter was granted by President Andrew Jackson in 1819.

By the late 1840s, Memphis was flourishing. The vision of dynamic river port, teeming with flatboats loaded with lumber, cotton, and other trade goods had come to pass. The river carried not only goods in and out of Memphis, however. Traders, peddlers, gamblers and other "river rats" streamed into Memphis, making hotel owners, saloon proprietors, and cotton merchants wealthy. Memphis became known as the "city of white gold," for the high quality cotton bought and sold there; fortunes were made on Front Street's "Cotton Row." Sadly, cotton was not the only commodity traded there. A marker known as the "Auction Block" still exists in downtown Memphis, marking the spot where enslaved peoples were bought, sold, and traded.

Memphis was federally occupied for two years during the Civil War, but was one of the few major southern cities that was not burned and looted during the war. In fact, Memphians profited from the war, selling cotton to one side, and then turning around selling gun powder, shoes, and other commodities to the other. By the end of the war, Memphis was the sixth largest city in the South, known more for its muddy, unpaved streets and lawlessness than its gentile citizenry.

Memphis' growth and development was curbed, however, not once but twice. In 1872 and again in 1878, Memphis experienced two yellow fever epidemics. The epidemics killed over 5,000 people and sent an additional 25,000 Memphians running to seek safety in other cities. Many never returned. The population fell dramatically, the city lost its charter, and was forced into bankruptcy.

Despite popular pressure that the city be abandoned and burned, Memphis rebounded. Money was raised through the sale of bonds to develop new city drainage and sanitation systems, and pave the constantly muddy streets. The population grew as money and ideas were pumped into the economy. By the turn of the century, the population of Memphis was more than 100,000, twice that of the pre-yellow fever decades.

Growth and development assured, largely due to the efforts of E.H. "Boss" Crump, Memphians turned to more leisurely pursuits.

Beale Street had long been the seedy destination for the citizenry that didn't fit into the economy of downtown, cotton row, or the stately mansions on "millionaires row." It was in these cramped streets, speak-easies, dance halls, and pool parlors that W. C. Handy found his "sound," and his audience. A black musician and composer, Handy is credited with establishing a truly American musical sound – the blues. This heady mix of gospel songs, spirituals, African music, and ragtime was a resounding success, and the sound spread throughout the city, state, and the entire south, as the more affluent took the sound as their own. The music took hold and once established, on Beale Street and throughout Memphis, the musical heritage of the area flourished to include jazz, blues, and eventually, rock and roll.

Today, Memphis is a thriving tourist destination, an important international distribution center and is in the midst of a multi-cultural renaissance of sorts. Tourists from all over the world flock to see historic Beale Street, and, of course, Graceland, Elvis Presley's home. In addition, the city has become a mecca for historians and tourists interested in immersing themselves in the history of the civil rights movement in the United States.

Memphis has matured into a vital city all the while maintaining its southern charm. What more needs to be said about a city that is known as the Home of the Blues *and* the Birthplace Rock and Roll, the beginnings of the self-serve supermarket as we know it (Piggly Wiggly), the best bar-b-que, the hottest music scene, the peabody ducks, not to mention the third largest pyramid in the world, and the worlds busiest international airport. Oh yes, and Elvis.

SOUVENIR OF THE SOUTH

Greetings from MEMPHIS, TENN.

Architecture

The architecture in Memphis is best described as mixed, with styles ranging from Federal, Greek Revival, Plantation Style, Traditional, Contemporary – a real myriad of styles. The Columbia Mutual Tower is a fine example of late Gothic Revival style, the Hellenic Orthodox Church is impressive – a Modified Byzantine style, and The Peabody Hotel, Italian Renaissance Revival.

Memphis boasts more than just impressive downtown architecture. Over 22,000 residents live in the central business district, enjoying a thriving urban lifestyle.

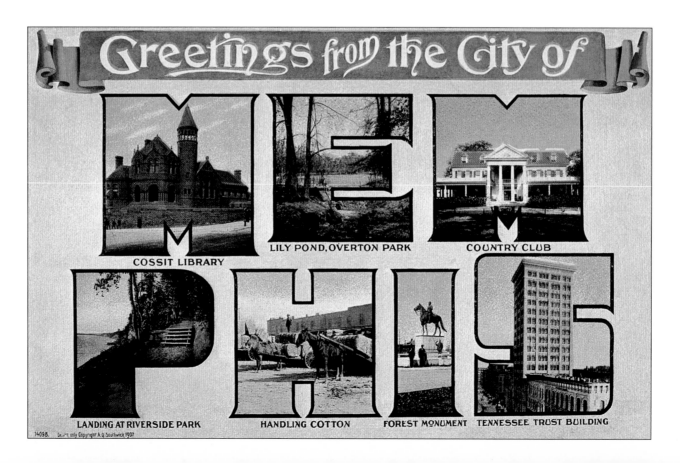

Greetings from the City of MEMPHIS

COSSIT LIBRARY — LILY POND, OVERTON PARK — COUNTRY CLUB — LANDING AT RIVERSIDE PARK — HANDLING COTTON — FOREST MONUMENT — TENNESSEE TRUST BUILDING

Street Scenes

BIRDS EYE VIEW NORTH. MEMPHIS, TENN.

MAIN STREET, MEMPHIS, TENN.-56

Colorful Main
Street, Memphis. The
Warner Brothers Theater on the right
is playing a Bette Davis film. [1940s era, $6-8]

Bird's eye views of Memphis show the
striking architecture throughout
downtown Memphis. [pre 1915, $8-10]

[Pre-1915, $7-9]

Birds Eye View. Memphis, Tenn.

Photo by Coovert.

Main Street Memphis welcomes you. [pre 1920, $8-10]

The lights of
Main Street. [pre
1915, $10-12]

Looking down Main Street,
the Gayoso Hotel is on the
left. [pre 1940s, $8-10]

Main Street, Memphis, teems with activity. Trolleys shuttle business men and women as well as shoppers between busy downtown streets. [pre 1915, $10-12]

From Court Square, Main Street looking south. [pre 1915, $10-12]

Looking
north on Main Street.
[pre 1915, $10-12]

A view of Main Street looking south from Poplar. Dinstuhl's is on the left.
[cancelled 1909, $10-12]

Main Street looking north from the Randolph building.
[cancelled 1908, $10-12]

A bustling Main Street north, from Madison Avenue. [pre 1915, $10-12]

Main Street North from Madison Avenue, Memphis, Tenn.

13549 SKYSCRAPER DISTRICT, MEMPHIS, TENN.

COPR J. C. COOVERT

[Pre 1920, $8-10]

In the Business District, Memphis, Tenn., on the Illinois Central System

[Linen era, $2-4]

Scene in Sky Scraper District,
Memphis, Tenn.

MADISON AVENUE EAST FROM TOWER OF CUSTOM HOUSE,
BY NIGHT, MEMPHIS, TENN.

The skyscrapers on Madison Avenue. The image was taken from the tower of the Custom House. Memphis had one of the most impressive downtowns at this time, especially at night. [pre 1915, $6-8]

The "skyscraper district," Memphis. At the time, Memphis' skyline was the most impressive in the South, a testament to industry and resilience. [pre 1915, $8-10]

Main Street and Madison. The crowds are evidence
of a thriving downtown economy. [pre 1920, $7-9]

[pre 1915, $8-10]

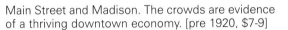

An impressive sight at the turn of the
century, looking west on Madison
Avenue, the Wall Street of Memphis. [pre 1920, $7-9]

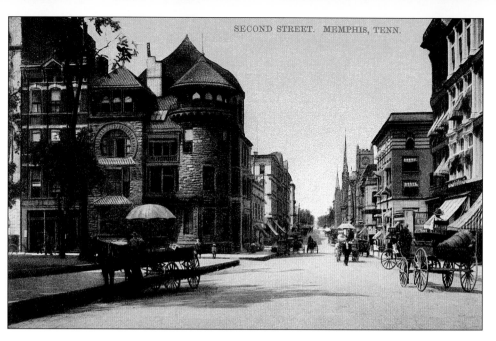

Second Street, Memphis. Horse and buggies still outnumber cars in this early view. [pre 1915, $8-10]

Looking up Madison Avenue. [pre-1915, $8-10]

Second Street looking south from Court Square. The proximity of the Mississippi River often caused fog, especially evidenced at night. [pre 1915, $8-10]

A rare aluminum postcard, showing Court Square, Memphis. [pre 1907, $15-20]

The back of the aluminum card, addressed but not posted.

Tennessee Trust
Building. [pre 1915, $5-7]
81 Madison Avenue.
National Register of Historic Places.

The Tennessee Trust
Building towers above a
bustling Main Street.
[pre 1915, $6-8]

Memphis Trust
Building. [pre 1920, $5-7]

Memphis Trust Building. [pre 1915, $5-7]

TENNESSEE TRUST BUILDING, MEMPHIS, TENN.

Tennessee Trust Building.
[pre 1915, $7-9]

COURT SQUARE FOUNTAIN AND
COLUMBIAN MUTUAL TOWER,
MEMPHIS, TENN.—50

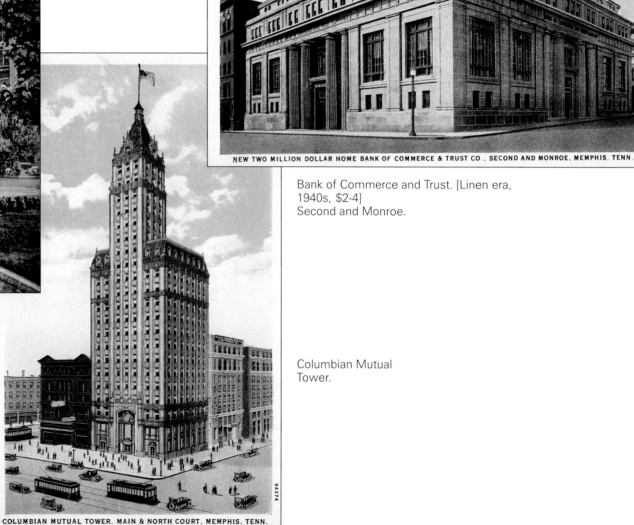

NEW TWO MILLION DOLLAR HOME BANK OF COMMERCE & TRUST CO., SECOND AND MONROE, MEMPHIS, TENN.

COLUMBIAN MUTUAL TOWER, MAIN & NORTH COURT, MEMPHIS, TENN.

Columbian Mutual Tower. [Linen era, 1940s, $2-4]
Corner of Main and North Court.
National Register of Historic Places.
Constructed in 1924, this building was designed by Boyer, Baum & Baum, and Isaac Albert, in the late gothic revival style. It is also known as the Lincoln American Tower.

Bank of Commerce and Trust. [Linen era, 1940s, $2-4]
Second and Monroe.

Columbian Mutual
Tower.

18

INTERIOR VIEW, BANK OF COMMERCE & TRUST COMPANY'S NEW T...

Bank of Commerce and Trust Company, interior. [White border era, $7-9]

UNION PLANTERS BANK BUILDING,

MISSISSIPPI RIVER IN THE BACKGROUND, MEMPHIS, TENN.   44

Union Planters Bank Building. The Mississippi River is in the background. [pre 1920, $5-7]

Advertising card from Bank of Commerce and Trust Co. [cancelled 1910, $8-10]

19

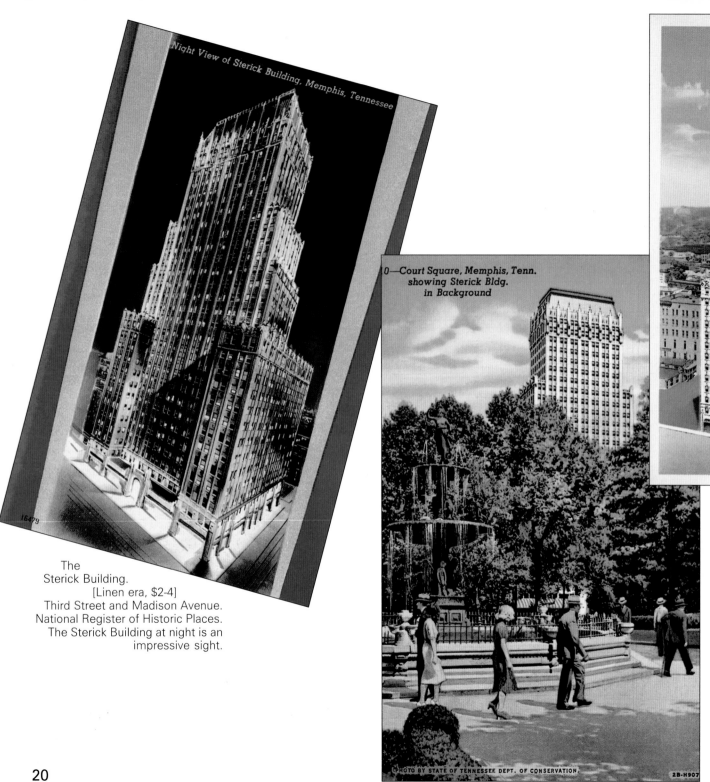

Night View of Sterick Building, Memphis, Tennessee

0—Court Square, Memphis, Tenn.
showing Sterick Bldg.
in Background

PHOTO BY STATE OF TENNESSEE DEPT. OF CONSERVATION.

Sterick Building, Memphis, Tenn.

The
Sterick Building.
[Linen era, $2-4]
Third Street and Madison Avenue.
National Register of Historic Places.
The Sterick Building at night is an
impressive sight.

The Sterick Tower, at twenty-nine
stories high, was the highest
building in the Memphis skyline
from 1930 to 1965. [Linen era, $2-4]

The Sterick Building towers over Court
Square. [Linen era, $2-4]

5346. Dr. Porter Building, Memphis, Tenn.

Dr. D.T. Porter Building. [pre 1915, $7-9]
Corner of Main and Court Avenues.
National Register of Historic Places.
Constructed in 1895, the Dr. D.T. Porter building
(formerly the Continental Bank building) was the city's
first steel-frame skyscraper. The Continental Bank
building was sold to the heirs of D.T. Porter who
renamed it to honor him, a former mayor during the
difficult yellow fever epidemic and taxing district times.
The Porter Building was the first building in Memphis to
boast an elevator.

Porter Building. [pre 1915, $7-9]

Dr. D.T. Porter Building. Memphis, Tenn.

Universal Life Insurance Company, Memphis, Tennessee

Universal Life Insurance Company. [Linen era, $2-4]
480 Linden Avenue at Wellington Street.

21

Public Buildings

Cossitt Library, Federal Building, and Post Office. [Linen era, $6-8] On April 12, 1893, the Cossitt Library, an impressive Romanesque, red sandstone building was dedicated.

COSSITT LIBRARY, FEDERAL BUILDING AND POST OFFICE, MEMPHIS, TENN.   1318

Cossett [sic] Library. [pre 1915, $4-6]

Series 1226 A.   Cossitt Library and Post Office, Memphis, Tenn.   Davidson Brothers.

An early view of the Cossitt Library and Post Office. Sadly, the buildings are no longer standing. [pre 1915, $4-6]

Memphis, Tenn. Cossett Library.

G 14634 Court House, Memphis, Tenn.

Court House. [pre 1915, $6-7]

Law Library, Court House, Memphis, Tenn.

Court House law library. [pre 1915, $5-7]

New Court House.
[pre 1915, $4-6]
Second, Third, Adams
and Washington
Avenues.

13022 New Court House, Memphis, Tenn.

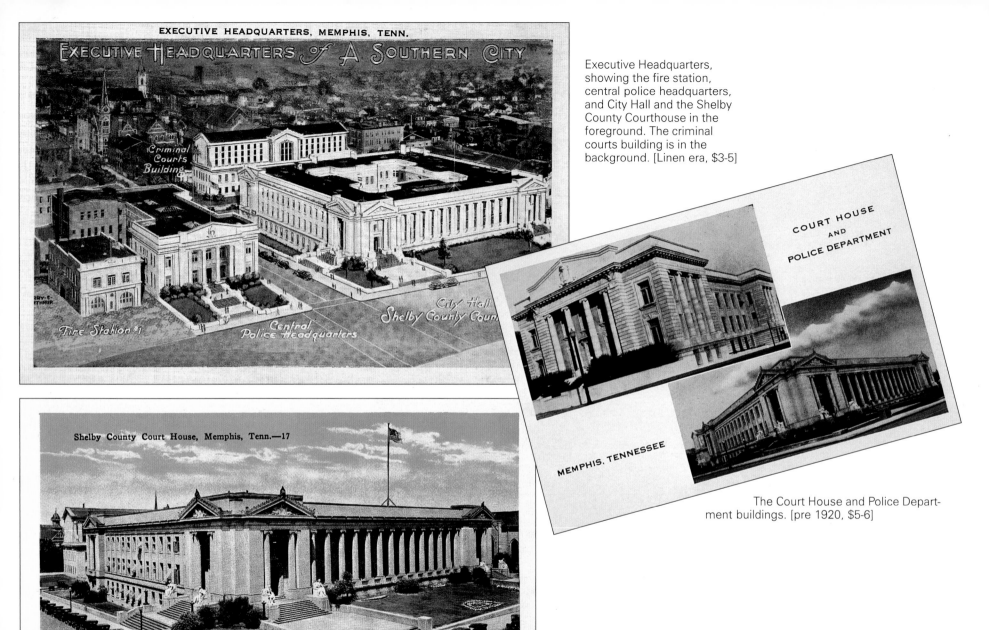

EXECUTIVE HEADQUARTERS, MEMPHIS, TENN.

EXECUTIVE HEADQUARTERS OF A SOUTHERN CITY

Criminal Courts Building

Fire Station #1

Central Police Headquarters

City Hall
Shelby County Cou...

Executive Headquarters, showing the fire station, central police headquarters, and City Hall and the Shelby County Courthouse in the foreground. The criminal courts building is in the background. [Linen era, $3-5]

COURT HOUSE AND POLICE DEPARTMENT

MEMPHIS, TENNESSEE

The Court House and Police Department buildings. [pre 1920, $5-6]

Shelby County Court House, Memphis, Tenn.—17

Shelby County Court House. [White Border era, $3-5]
193-205 N. Main.
From the back: "Shelby County Courthouse, one of the finest examples of architecture among the public buildings of the south. The City Hall is maintained in the Court House, which also houses city, and county offices, the circuit, chancery, county and probate courts, the Law Library, the city and county health boards, and the county school board. Criminal courts are housed in the new Criminal courts and jail building north of the Courthouse."

COTTON EXCHANGE. MEMPHIS, TENN.

[Pre 1915, $8-10]

Memphis, Tenn. Cotton Exchange.

2533.

Memphis Cotton Exchange Building. [pre 1915, $5-7]
Second and Madison Ave.
The Exchange Building, completed in 1910, once housed the Cotton and
Merchant Exchanges where fortunes were won and lost.

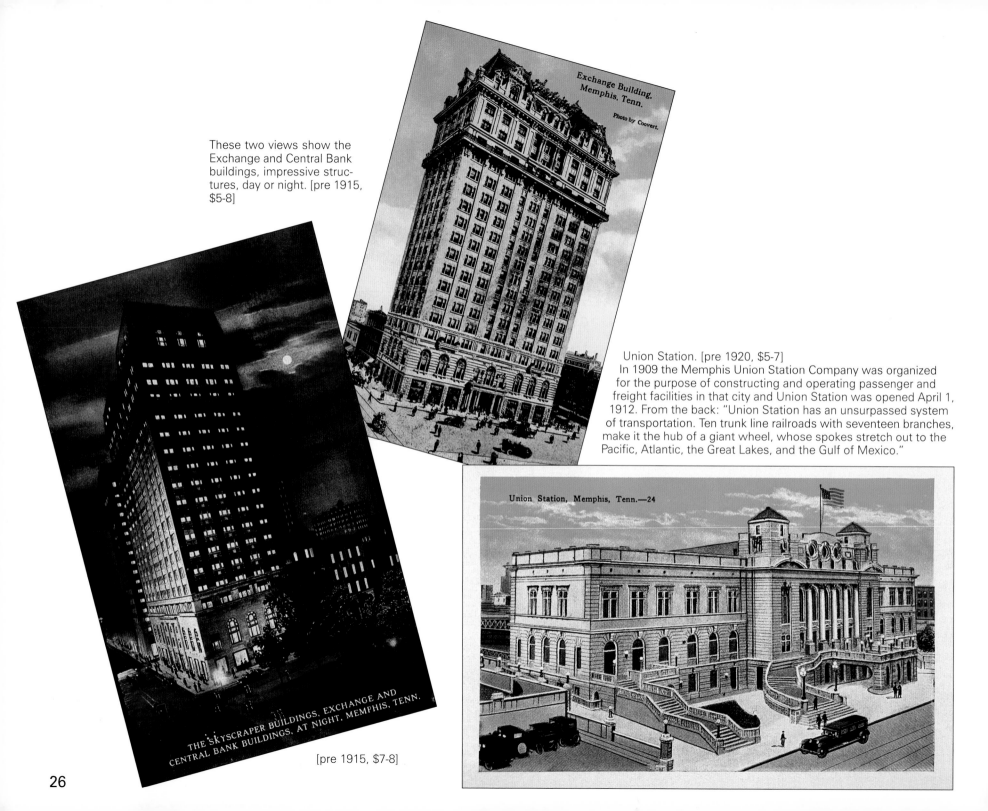

These two views show the Exchange and Central Bank buildings, impressive structures, day or night. [pre 1915, $5-8]

Exchange Building, Memphis, Tenn.
Photo by Coovert.

Union Station. [pre 1920, $5-7]
In 1909 the Memphis Union Station Company was organized for the purpose of constructing and operating passenger and freight facilities in that city and Union Station was opened April 1, 1912. From the back: "Union Station has an unsurpassed system of transportation. Ten trunk line railroads with seventeen branches, make it the hub of a giant wheel, whose spokes stretch out to the Pacific, Atlantic, the Great Lakes, and the Gulf of Mexico."

THE SKYSCRAPER BUILDINGS, EXCHANGE AND CENTRAL BANK BUILDINGS, AT NIGHT, MEMPHIS, TENN.

[pre 1915, $7-8]

Union Station, Memphis, Tenn.—24

Barksdale Mounted Police Station,
Memphis, Tenn.

A rare view of the Barksdale Mounted Police outside the
Barksdale Police Station. [pre 1915, $12-15]

Memphis, Tenn.
Central Fire Station.

Central fire station.
[cancelled 1908, $12-15]

27

5349. Custom House, Memphis, Tenn.

Federal Building. [cancelled 1910, $4-6]

14076 – Federal Building Memphis Tenn

Memphis, Tenn.

2589.

Custom House.

[pre 1915, $4-6]

[Pre 1915, $4-6]

28

Shelby County Court House, Memphis, Tenn.

Copyrighted 1910 by Coovert.

Shelby County Courthouse. [pre 1915, $3-5]

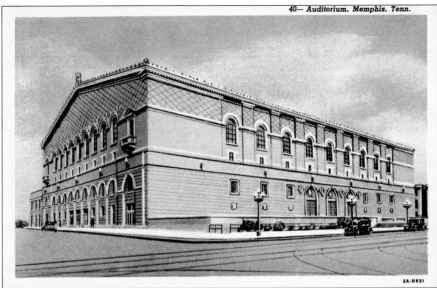

40— Auditorium, Memphis, Tenn.

13— United States Custom House, Court House
and Post Office, Memphis, Tenn.

United States Custom House, Court House, and Post Office. [Linen era, $2-4]
Madison Avenue.

MUNICIPAL AUDITORIUM, MEMPHIS, TENN.—16

Municipal Auditorium. [Linen era, $2-4]
From the back: "Municipal Auditorium, a $3,000,000 structure built by
the City of Memphis and Shelby County. The auditorium occupies an
entire block in the heart of downtown. Its mammoth amphitheatre seats
12,500. It can be divided into two halls, one for 6,500 and the other for
2,500. There are excellent facilities for entertaining great national
conventions. The stage is one of the largest in the country."

44—*Administration Building, Memphis Municipal Airport, Memphis, Tenn.*

OB-H1249

Beale Street Market House.
[pre 1915, $7-9]

Memphis, Tenn. Beal St., Market House.

Administration Building, Memphis Municipal Airport. [Linen era, $5-7]
From the back: "The Memphis Municipal Airport is one of the finest in the country."

Memphis, Tenn.   Randolph Bldg.

Randolph Building. [pre
1915, $5-7]
South Main St.

2538.

Falls Building, Memphis, Tenn.

13283 Commercial Appeal Building,
Memphis, Tenn.

Commercial Appeal Building. [pre 1915, $5-7]

Falls Building.[pre 1915, $5-8]

Goodwin Institute, Memphis, T

The Elizabeth Club. [pre 1915, $4-6]
360 Carroll Avenue.

Shrine Building.
[1920s, $4-6]

Goodwin Institute. [cancelled 1914, $4-6]

Elks Club. [pre 1915, $4-6]
Jefferson Avenue.

The Rex Club and
Y.M.H.A. [pre 1915,
$4-6]
Second and Adams
Avenues.

Y.M.C.A. Building. [pre 1920, $3-5]
177 Union Ave.
The YMCA of Memphis purchased property on
the south side of Madison near Fourth and built a
seven story structure in 1909. The building was
formally dedicated by William Howard Taft, then
President-elect of the United States, along with
the governors of twenty-seven other states.

Tennessee Club. [1906, $4-6]
Court Avenue.

University Center. [Linen era, $2-4]
Madison and Dunlap.

Y.W.C.A. Building. [pre 1920, $3-5]

Goldsmith & Sons Co. [pre 1920, $4-6]
South Main St.
The store with better values, serving Memphis since 1870.
Goldsmith's became a true department store, among the first in the South, when it arranged merchandise by departments in 1902. It was the first Memphis store to install air-conditioning, escalators, a bargain basement, and a mechanical credit system. Goldsmith's also initiated a Christmas parade, preceding Macy's famous event by more than a decade.

Goldsmith's, *Greater Memphis' Greatest Store.* [Linen era, $2-4]

[Linen era, $2-4]

J. GOLDSMITH & SONS CO. THE STORE OF BETTER VALUES, SERVING MEMPHIS SINCE, 1870.

GOLDSMITH'S — MEMPHIS' GREATEST STORE

35

Bry's Department Store. [pre 1920, $6-8]
N. Main Street and Jefferson.
Memphis' Leading Department Store.

Lowensteins Department Store.
[pre 1920, $6-8]
National Register of Historic Places.
From the back: "An unusual department
store serving Memphis and the Mid-South
since 1855."

Bry's Department Store.
[cancelled 1904, $4-6]
An upscale department store; in
addition to shopping, Bry's
featured areas for dining, beauty
parlours, and first class ladies
rest rooms.

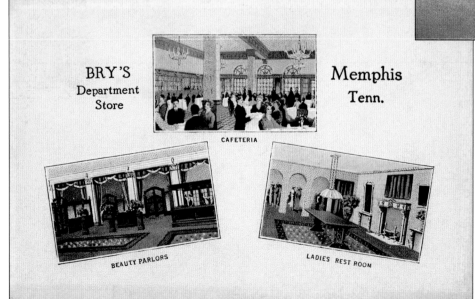

Sears, Roebuck & Company, Memphis, Tenn.

Sears, Roebuck, and Company. [Linen era, $3-5]
Corner of Watkins and North Parkway.
From the back: "One of the largest and most impressive structures in Memphis and the Mid South, located on a spacious tract of land at the corner of Watkins and North Parkway which provides parking facilities of over 1,000 cars."

Flour Mill, Memphis, Tenn.

Flour Mill.
[cancelled
1910, $6-8]

Linden Station-Wholesale District, Memphis, Tenn.

Linden Station – Wholesale District.
[cancelled 1909, $6-8]
Beale Street Landing.
National Register of Historic Places.

Greyhound Bus Terminal. [Linen era, $4-6]

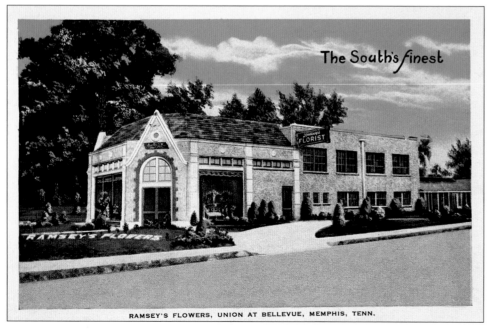

Tri State Floral Co. [Linen era, $6-8]
1403 Union Ave.
From the back: "Successfully growing and
selling flowers to Memphis since 1880."

Ramsey's Flowers.
[Linen era, $6-8]
Union Avenue at
Bellevue.

McLellens. [Linen era, $6-8]
South Main St.

McLELLAN'S

South Main Street, Memphis, Tenn.   4B-H1367

HOME OF MEMPHIS STEAM LAUNDRY, MEMPHIS, TENN.   111188

Advertising card for Memphis Steam Laundry. [pre 1920, $6-8]

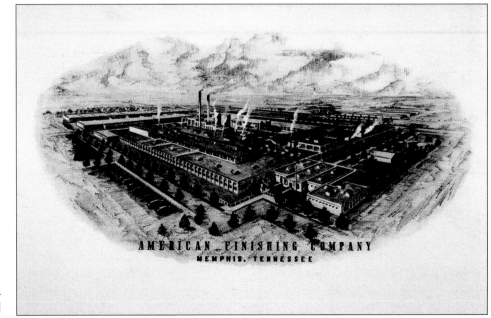

AMERICAN FINISHING COMPANY
MEMPHIS, TENNESSEE

American Finishing Company. [pre 1915, $8-10]

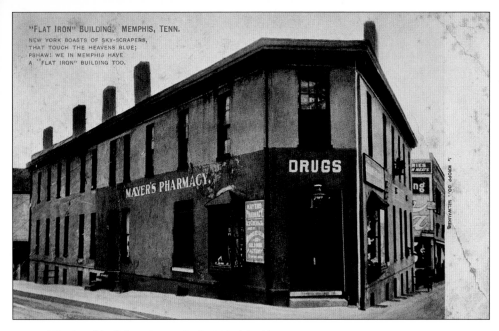

"Flat Iron" building. [cancelled 1908, $8-10]
Verse: *New York boasts of sky-scrapers, that touch the heavens blue; Pshaw! We in Memphis have a "Flat Iron" building too.*

Memphis Paper Co. [cancelled 1916, $6-8]
The largest paper warehouse in the south.
From the back: "Capital $1,000,000 – rated "A1"
(Excellent) in Dunne's International Insurance Report."

Barnes & Miller Hardware
Co. [pre 1915, $8-10]

Southern Bowling Lanes. [Linen era, $2-4]
299 Cleveland St.
From the back: "The Bowling Palace of America,
represents the ultimate in the modern trend in the Ten
Pin Game. 24 Streamline Burnswick Drives, equipped
with Tele-fowl [sic], Tele-score. Seating capacity 500."

SOUTHERN BOWLING LANES — 299 CLEVELAND ST. — MEMPHIS, TENN.

Fortunes Incorporated.
[Linen era, $8-10]
Union Avenue and
Belvedere Blvd.
Manufacturers of "all-
cream ice cream."

41

First Hotel in Memphis before the war. [cancelled 1909, $8-10]

From the back: "The South's Finest – One of America's
Best – 625 Rooms – 625 Baths." [Linen era, $2-4]

Peabody Hotel, in the heart of the business, shopping,
and skyscraper district of the city. [pre 1920, $4-6]

Hotel Peabody. [pre 1920, $3-5]
149 Union Avenue.

THIRD AND MADISON LOOKING SOUTH,

SHOWING NEW PEABODY HOTEL, MEMPHIS, TENN

112637

[pre 1920, $4-6]

13277
Peabody Hotel,
Memphis, Tenn.

Built shortly after the Civil War, the Peabody Hotel is an American Institution. Its luxurious lobby features crystal chandeliers, enormous floral arrangements, and impressive Italian Renaissance Revival architecture. [pre 1915, $10-12]

Front and back of advertising card – the front advertises the new Peabody Hotel, while the back shows a photograph of the Gayoso Hotel. [pre 1915, $4-6]

MEMPHIS HAS A NEW MILLION DOLLAR HOTEL

THE PEABODY HOTEL

Brand new, a modern hotel in every sense of the word, was quietly opened to the public on the evening of March 5th. Have you visited

The Beautiful Cafes opening Directly upon Main Street

Or inspected the delightful rooms, handsomely furnished? The Management will be glad to have you do so. We desire to furnish the very best restaurant service possible, at the most reasonable rates.

RATES FOR ROOMS, HOT AND COLD WATER, LONG DISTANCE TELEPHONE, ETC., IN EVERY ROOM, $1.50 PER DAY AND UPWARD.

WRITE OR ASK FOR INFORMATION.

English Breakfast Room, Peabody Hotel. [cancelled 1915, $8-10]

LOBBY, HOTEL PEABODY, MEMPHIS.

106189

Lobby of the Hotel Peabody, showing the famous fountain in the center. [pre 1920, $5-7]

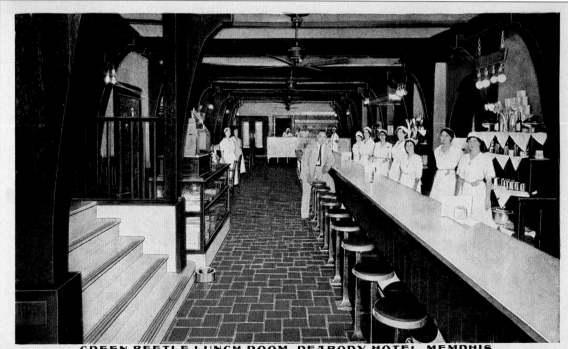

THE LOBBY, HOTEL PEABODY, MEMPHIS, TENN.

The lobby of the famous Peabody Hotel. [pre 1920, $6-8]

Green Beetle Lunch Room, Peabody Hotel. [pre 1915, $10-12]

GREEN BEETLE LUNCH ROOM, PEABODY HOTEL, MEMPHIS.
BEST PLACE IN CITY FOR A SPLENDID MEAL AT A MODERATE PRICE.
TABLE SERVICE FOR LADIES AND GENTLEMEN.

Ladies Parlor, Peabody Café, Peabody Hotel. [pre 1915, $10-12]

Venetian Room, Main Cafe of the Peobody Hotel. As its name implies, the room was ornately decorated with gold accents. [pre 1920, $6-8]

Rip Van Winkle Grill, Peabody Hotel. [pre 1920, $6-8]

Gayoso Hotel. [pre 1915, $6-8]

The Famous Peabody Ducks. [pre 1915, $6-8]
As opulent as it is, the main attraction of the Peabody is the twice-daily march of the Peabody Ducks. At 11:00am each morning they descend from their penthouse, down a red carpet, and into the hotel lobby's ornate fountain; at 5:00pm, they reverse their trip, march up the red carpet to the elevator and retire for the night. The present ducks are direct descendants of the original Mallard ducks placed in the fountain when the hotel was opened in 1869.

Advertising card for the Peabody Hotel. [pre 1915, $4-6]

Gayoso Hotel. [cancelled 1909, $6-8].
Main Street

Hotel Gayoso. [pre 1915, $6-8]
From the back: "To occupy a room in a fire-proof building, to have hot and cold running water, long distance telephones, a room cleaned by sanitary methods, and handsomely furnished, with bath and toilet facilities, if desired. To have the advantage of the service, the beautiful parlors, and lounging spaces of a modern hotel, and how much is the difference in price?"

Gayoso Hotel. [cancelled 1910, $6-8]

Rear Hotel Gayoso – an impressive sight. [pre 1915, $6-8]

The drawing room
of the Hotel Gayoso is
spacious and features a grand piano.
[pre 1920, $4-6]

Hotel Gayoso. [Linen era, $6-8]
From the back: "Famous for Years. 300 rooms, reasonable rates. C.C. Cartwright, Pres. and General Manager."

Hotel Chisca. [Linen era, $2-4]

Hotel Chisca. [Linen era, $2-4]
Built in 1913, the Hotel Chisca was one of the premier hotels in Memphis at the time, boasting "traditional Southern cooking," air conditioned guest rooms, and banquet facilities for all occasions.

Lobby, Hotel Chisca. [pre 1920, $6-8]

Hotel Claridge. [pre 1920, $3-5]
Main at Adams.
National Register of Historic Places.

The Hotel Claridge. [pre 1915, $4-6]
From the back: "Six floors completely air conditioned. Dining and dancing nightly. 20th century room and star-light roof garden."

Hotel Claridge. [Linen era, $2-4]

IN THE HEART OF DOWNTOWN
SAINT LOUIS

HOTEL CLARIDGE

350 ROOMS
LOCUST AT EIGHTEENTH, ST. LOUIS
IN THE CENTER OF THE WHOLESALE DISTRICT

HOTEL MARK TWAIN

300 ROOMS
EIGHTH AND PINE

HOME OF THE FAMOUS
STR. MARK TWAIN
COFFEE SHOP

HOTEL CLARIDGE

400 ROOMS
MAIN AT ADAMS ST., MEMPHIS, TENN.
SERVIDOR SERVICE IN EVERY ROOM

HOTEL CLARIDGE -- "The South's Smart Hotel" -- MEMPHIS, TENN.

CASCADES ROOF GARDEN

20TH CENTURY ROOM

HOTEL CLARIDGE -- MEMPHIS, TENN.

6A-H1481

The Hotel Claridge, Memphis (right) as well as two locations in St. Louis. This fine hotel advertised "guest rooms with tub and shower, circulating ice water, and electric fan. [pre 1915, $6-8]

"The South's Smartest Hotel," the Hotel Claridge. [Linen era, $2-4]

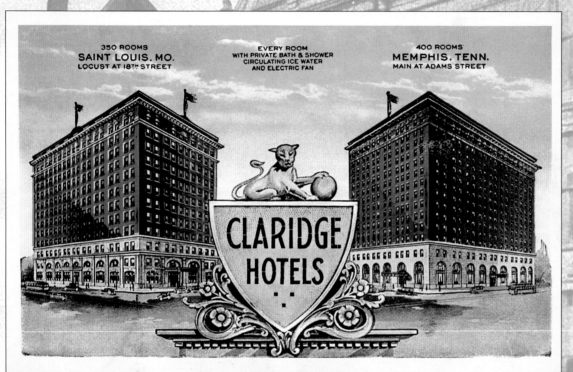

Hotel Claridge. [pre 1920, $4-6]

350 ROOMS
SAINT LOUIS, MO.
LOCUST AT 18TH STREET

EVERY ROOM
WITH PRIVATE BATH & SHOWER
CIRCULATING ICE WATER
AND ELECTRIC FAN

400 ROOMS
MEMPHIS, TENN.
MAIN AT ADAMS STREET

CLARIDGE HOTELS

Hotel King Cotton. [Linen era, $2-4]
North Front Street and Jefferson Avenue.
Air conditioning was a commodity, as was plenty of available parking,
that attracted guests. Sadly this building has been demolished.

Lobby of the King Cotton Hotel. [Linen era, $4-6] From the back: "Every room with private bath, running ice water, three channels of radio and Musak. Large Banquet rooms and Coffee Shop." "Home of the Army-Navy Club."

Lobby, King Cotton Hotel, Memphis, Tenn.

Alcazar. [cancelled 1915, $6-8] Corner of Adams and Fourth.

"Alcazar," corner of Adams and Fourth, one block from car line, Memphis, Tenn.

55

Hotel William Len. [Linen era, $2-4]
Monroe St.

William Len Hotel. [Linen era, $2-4]
The William Len was at one time considered one of the
finest hotels in Memphis. It had fallen into disrepair,
was used as an apartment residence, and abandoned
for a time. A major renovation project undertaken by
the Marriott Corporation has preserved much of the
original Art Deco feeling of the façade.

Hotel De Voy. [Linen era, $2-4]
Corner of Jefferson and Front St.
A popularly priced hotel, the Hotel DeVoy catered to the
cost-conscious guest with the slogan "Sleep in safety
and comfort without extravagance."

HOTEL TENNESSEE
MEMPHIS, TENN.

HOTEL TENNESSEE, MEMPHIS, TENN.

1045

The Hotel Tennessee is an impressive sight. [Linen era, $2-4]

Hotel Tennessee. [Linen era, $2-4]
Third and Union.

Parkview Hotel. [pre 1920, $3-5]
A later card advertised "Parkview Apartment
Hotel - a beautiful new structure with every
modern convenience."

Parkview Hotel, Memphis, Tenn.—7

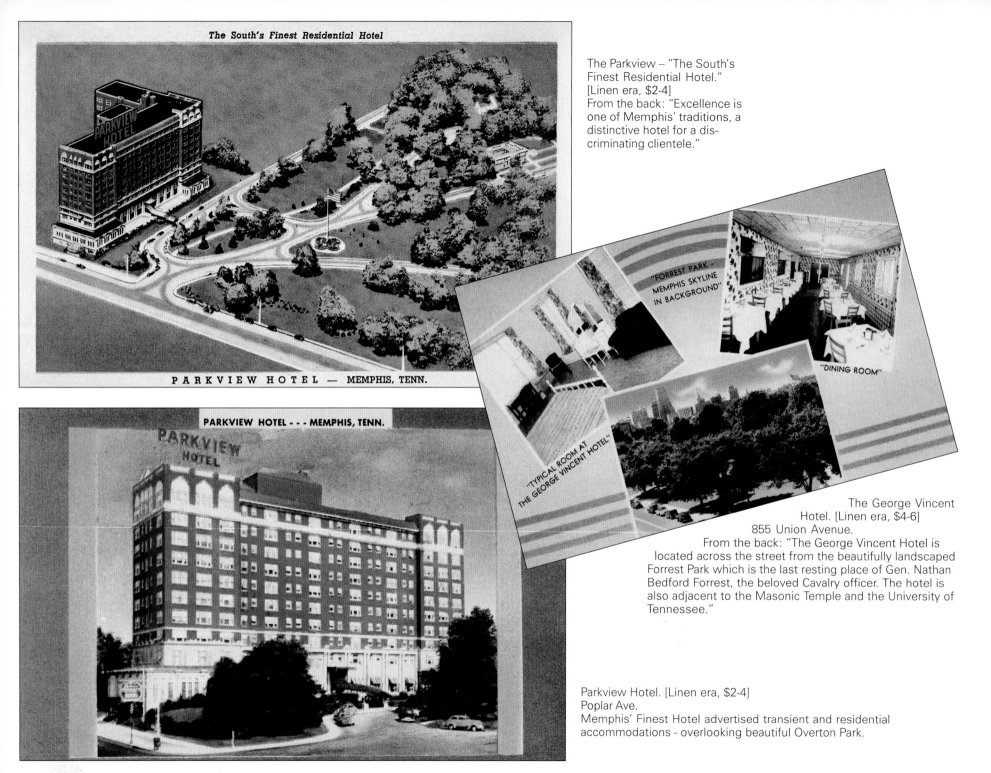

The South's Finest Residential Hotel

PARKVIEW HOTEL — MEMPHIS, TENN.

PARKVIEW HOTEL - - - MEMPHIS, TENN.

PARKVIEW HOTEL

"FORREST PARK - MEMPHIS SKYLINE IN BACKGROUND"

"DINING ROOM"

"TYPICAL ROOM AT THE GEORGE VINCENT HOTEL"

The Parkview – "The South's Finest Residential Hotel." [Linen era, $2-4] From the back: "Excellence is one of Memphis' traditions, a distinctive hotel for a discriminating clientele."

The George Vincent Hotel. [Linen era, $4-6] 855 Union Avenue. From the back: "The George Vincent Hotel is located across the street from the beautifully landscaped Forrest Park which is the last resting place of Gen. Nathan Bedford Forrest, the beloved Cavalry officer. The hotel is also adjacent to the Masonic Temple and the University of Tennessee."

Parkview Hotel. [Linen era, $2-4] Poplar Ave. Memphis' Finest Hotel advertised transient and residential accommodations - overlooking beautiful Overton Park.

58

Christmas Display at The George Vincent Hotel
855 Union Ave., Memphis, Tennessee

This display was a part of the George Vincent Hotel for many years. The papier-mache Nativity display was designed and created by H.M. Phipps, a prominent Memphis artist. [Linen era, $4-6]

PLAZA HOTEL — MEMPHIS' FINEST COLORED HOTEL

HOTEL QUEEN ANNE—LARGEST COLORED HOTEL IN MEMPHIS

The Plaza Hotel. [Linen era, $8-10]
214 East Calhoun (opposite Union Station).
This was advertised as "Memphis' finest colored hotel," and a prominent sign displayed "Plaza Hotel: Colored Operated."

The Hotel Queen Anne. [Linen era, $8-10]
Vance at Third St.
A "colored only" hotel, the Queen Anne billed itself as the "Largest colored hotel in Memphis."

FORREST PARK HOTEL APARTMENTS—OPPOSITE FORREST PARK

Forrest Park Hotel Apartments. [Linen era, $2-4]
Madison and Court at Manassas St.
The Forrest Park Hotel, which featured daily, weekly, and monthly rentals, billed itself as the cleanest, completely furnished hotel in Memphis. Another draw was its location "out of congested district, yet convenient to Business Center."

BERRYMAN'S TOURIST COURT — HIGHWAY 61, SOUTH — MEMPHIS, TENN.

A SHOW PLACE OF MEMPHIS

6A-H2759

J.C. HARBIN'S TOURIST COTTAGES
Easy to find
MEMPHIS, TENN.
U.S. 51 SOUTH
Fine Food · Beautyrest Mattresses
Swimming Pool · Baths · Steam & Gas Heat
J.C. HARBIN

J.C. Harbin's Tourist Cottages. [Linen era, $10-12]
Highway 51 South.
Advertising "Fine Food, Beautyrest Mattresses, Swimming Pool, Baths, Steam and Gas Heat" these tourist cottages catered to families on vacation.

Berryman's Tourist Court. [cancelled 1949, $4-6]
Highway 61, South.

HI-WAY TOURIST HOME

1268 UNION AVE. — DIRECTLY OPPOSITE METHODIST HOSPITAL — MEMPHIS, TENN.   9B-H1687

Hi-Way Tourist Home. [Linen era, $3-4]
1268 Union Avenue.
This beautiful old Victorian Home was turned into a tourist home. It was located directly across from the Methodist Hospital, just seven minutes from the shopping district, and two blocks from Crump Stadium. [cancelled 1950]

Leahy's Tourist Court. [Linen era, $4-6]
3070 Summer Ave.
This small all-cottage motel boasts modern amenities and 100% air-conditioned rooms.

[Linen era, $4-6]

LEAHY'S TOURIST COURT - 3070 SUMMER AVE. - - MEMPHIS, TENN.

61

Bellevue Baptist Church, Memphis, Tennessee

[pre 1920, $4-6]

BELLEVUE BAPTIST CHURCH, MEMPHIS, TENNESSEE

Bellevue Baptist Church
N. Bellevue Blvd. [Linen era, $2-4]

UNION AVENUE BAPTIST CHURCH — MEMPHIS, TENNESSEE   3B-H1352

Union Avenue Baptist Church. [Linen era, $2-4]
Corner of Union Avenue and Summit.
From the back: "The church building, completed in 1942, has auditorium seating capacity of eighteen hundred, and education and social equipment consisting of more than a hundred rooms, modern offices, kitchen and dining room facilities."

UNION AVENUE BAPTIST CHURCH — MEMPHIS, TENNESSEE

Union Avenue Baptist
Church. [Linen era, $2-4]
Union and Summitt Avenues.

Central Baptist Church,
Memphis, Tenn.

Central Baptist Church.
[pre-1915, $4-6]

McLean Baptist Church.
[Linen era, $2-4]
815 N. McLean.
From the back: "This church is
now under construction and
when completed, the lovely
sanctuary will provide seating
facilities for 1,275. McLean
Baptist Church is known as
the church with a great future
and hard at work today."

McLean Baptist Church
815 N. McLean   Memphis, Tenn.

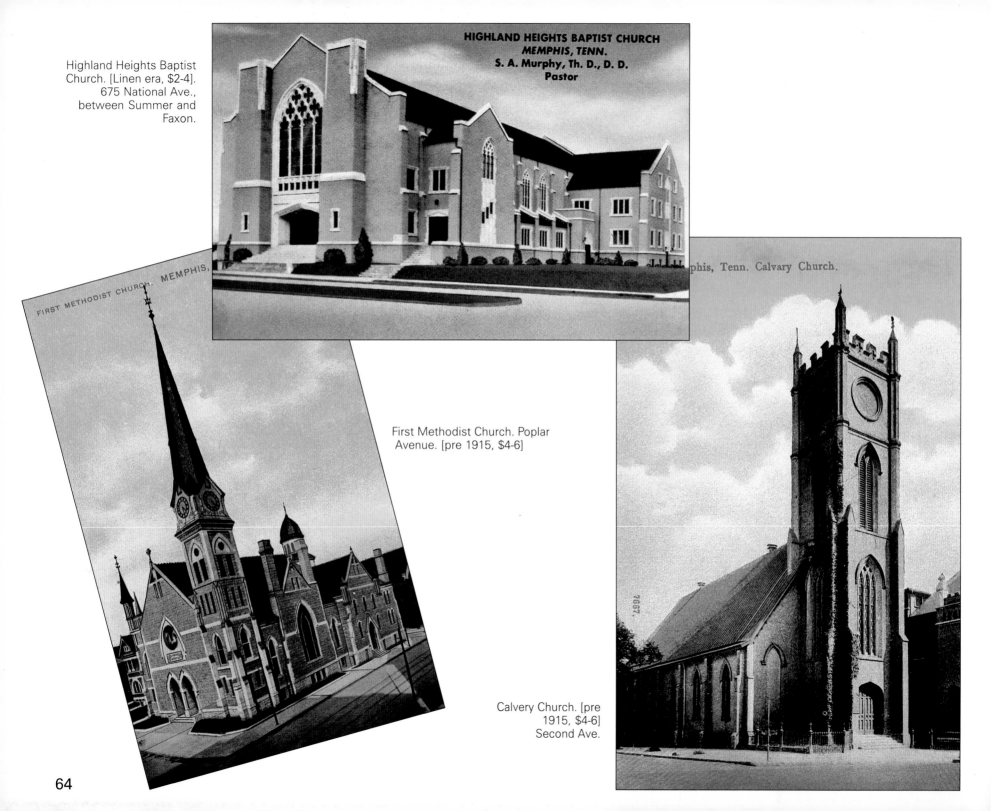

Highland Heights Baptist Church. [Linen era, $2-4]. 675 National Ave., between Summer and Faxon.

HIGHLAND HEIGHTS BAPTIST CHURCH
MEMPHIS, TENN.
S. A. Murphy, Th. D., D. D.
Pastor

...phis, Tenn. Calvary Church.

FIRST METHODIST CHURCH, MEMPHIS,

First Methodist Church. Poplar Avenue. [pre 1915, $4-6]

Calvery Church. [pre 1915, $4-6] Second Ave.

First Methodist Church, Memphis, Tennessee
"Memphis Methodism's Mother Church"

First Methodist Church. [pre 1940, $2-4]
From the back: "First Methodist Church, Memphis Methodism's Mother Church. Organized as a Methodist Society in 1826 with three members: first church in this city, then a sprawling Village on the Mississippi. In 1832, the Old Meeting House, first church building in Memphis - a log building with split log seats - was erected. From this small beginning First Methodist Church and Methodism have grown large."

Second Methodist Church. [Cancelled 1908, $4-6]

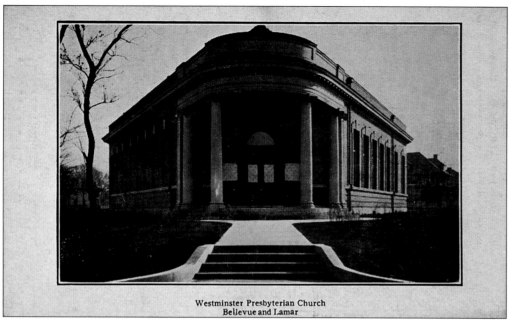

Westminster Presbyterian Church. [pre 1915, $4-6]
Bellevue and Lamar.

IDLEWILD PRESBYTERIAN CHURCH, MEMPHIS, TENN.

Idlewild Presbyterian
Church.
Union Ave. [pre 1920,
$3-5]

Evergreen Presbyterian
Church. [1930s, $3-5]

1st Presbyterian Church,
Memphis, Tenn.

1st Presbyterian Church.
Poplar Ave. and Third St. [pre 1915, $4-6]

St. Mary's Church and School.
Market Ave. and Third St.
[pre 1915, $4-6]

St. Mary's Cathedral, Memphis, Tenn.

St. Mary's Cathedral.
[pre 1915, $4-6]

ST. PETERS, ADAMS AVE. MEMPHIS, TENN.

St. Peters Catholic
Church [cancelled
1912, $4-6]
Adams Avenue

Tenn. St. Peter's Catholic Church.

St. Peters Catholic Church.
[cancelled 1907, $4-6]

Interior, St. Peter's Catholic
Church. [pre 1915, $4-6]

ST. PETER'S CATHOLIC CHURCH, ADAMS AND THIRD STREETS, MEMPHIS, TENN.

ST. PETERS ORPHANAGE, MEMPHIS, TENN.

St. Peter's Orphanage.
McLean Blvd. and Poplar Ave. [pre 1920, $3-5]

Immaculate Conception Church, Memphis, Tenn.

8A-H1641

Immaculate Conception Church.
[Linen era, $2-4]
The church was completed in 1938,
and at the time, was the largest
Catholic Church in Memphis.

MEMPHIS, Tenn.
St. Patrick's
Church.

St. Patrick's Catholic Church. [pre 1915, $4-6]
Linden Ave.
From the back: "St. Patrick's church is
conspicuous even among the many hand-
some church edifices which the city supports.
The property of the Roman Catholics, the
Church, both as to the exterior and interior, is
most impressive, and the congregation the
largest and wealthiest in the city.

69

Immaculate Conception Church.
[Linen era, $4-6]
1695 Central Avenue.

St. Joseph Church. [Linen era, $2-4]
135 St. Paul St.

Our Lady of Grace Shrine, St. Thomas Church. [pre 1915, $3-5] Memphis' temperate climate is responsible for the lush plantings around the shrine.

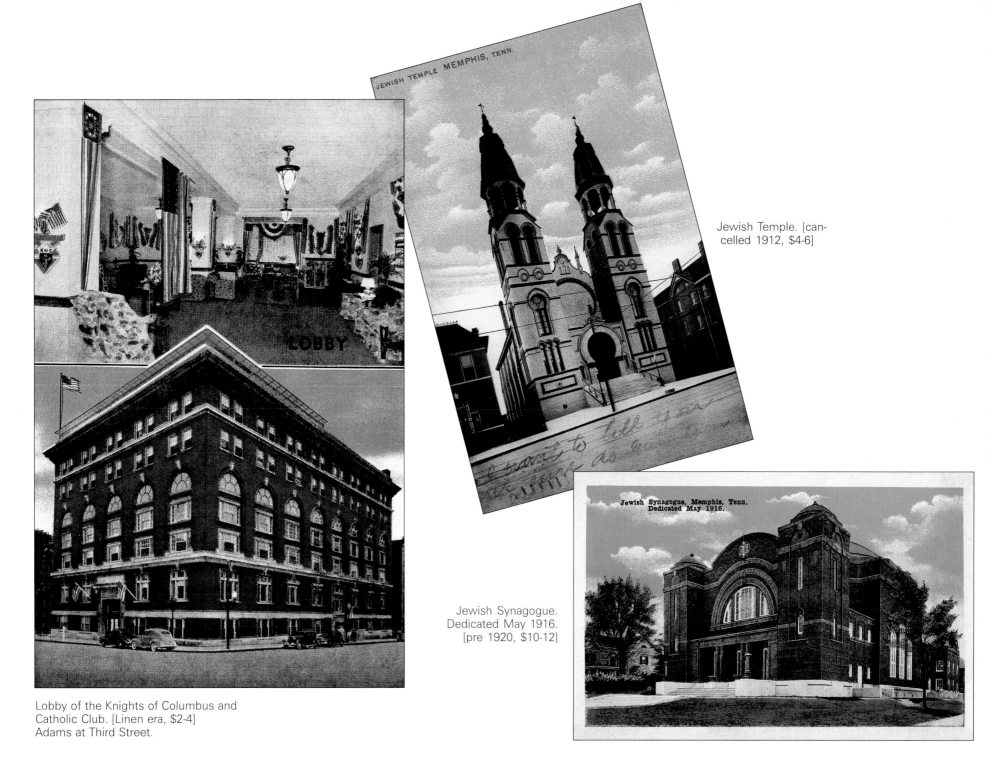

JEWISH TEMPLE MEMPHIS, TENN.

Jewish Temple. [cancelled 1912, $4-6]

Jewish Synagogue, Memphis, Tenn.
Dedicated May 1916.

Jewish Synagogue.
Dedicated May 1916.
[pre 1920, $10-12]

Lobby of the Knights of Columbus and
Catholic Club. [Linen era, $2-4]
Adams at Third Street.

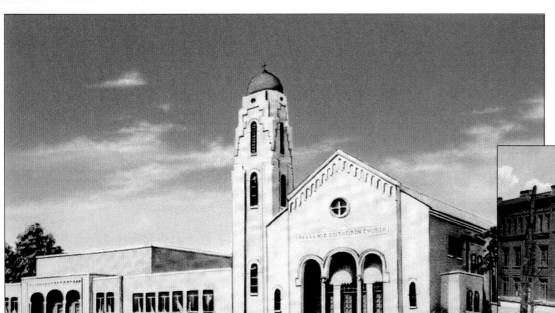

Hellenic Orthodox Church. [Linen era, $2-4]
Highland & Galloway Ave.
The church, designed in a modified Byzantine style
is of solid masonry construction.

Masonic Temple. [cancelled 1910, $4-6]
Court Ave. and Fourth St.
Home of the several Blue Lodges in
Memphis, it also houses the Eastern Star
and the Knights Templar.

Tennessee Consistory No. 1 Scottish Rite
Masonic Cathedral. [pre 1915, $4-6]
Dunlap St. and Union Ave.
Home of the Scottish Rite bodies of Tennes-
see. It contains one of the most magnificent
pipe organs in the south.

MASONIC TEMPLE, MEMPHIS. TENN.

SCOTTISH RITE CATHEDRAL, MEMPHIS, TENN.

Scottish Rite Cathedral, Memphis, Tenn.

Scottish Rite Cathedral. [cancelled 1913, $6-8]

The Masonic Temple and
Scottish Rite Cathedral.
[pre 1920, $6-8]

New Masonic Temple,
Memphis, Tenn.

First Church of Christ Scientist, Memphis, Tenn.

First Church of Christ Scientist. [pre 1915, $6-8]
Union Ave., near Wellington.

New Masonic Temple.
[pre 1920, $6-8]

Hospitals

Methodist Hospital, Memphis, Tenn.—8

Methodist Hospital. [pre 1920, $4-6]
1265 Union Avenue.
From the back: "One of the largest and best equipped institutions owned by the Southern Methodist Church, the hospital received a "Class A" rating by the American College of Surgeons."

World War Veterans Hospital, Memphis, Tenn.—14

World War Veterans Hospital. [pre 1920, $4-6]
1025 Lamar Boulevard.
From the back: "Modern in every detail, the hospital provides for the comfort and healthcare needs of World War veterans who paid the price of victory with their health and strength."

St. Joseph's Hospital, Memphis, Tenn.—9

St. Joseph's Hospital. [pre 1920, $4-6]
264 Jackson Ave.
From the back: "St. Joseph's Hospital, Catholic Institution associated with the growth and humanitarian work of Memphis. Has recently had a $400,000 wing added. Is rated as a "Class A" Hospital."

U.S. WAR VETERANS' HOSPITAL, MEMPHIS, TENN.—28

U.S. War Veterans Hospital. [pre 1920, $4-6]
1025 Lamar Boulevard.
National Register of Historic Places.

Tri-State Baptist Memorial Hospital, Memphis, Tenn.

Tri-State Baptist Memorial Hospital. [pre 1920, $4-6]

5— Baptist Hospital, Memphis, Tenn.

OB-H1247

Baptist Memorial Hospital. [Linen era, $2-4]
From the back: "The South's greatest hospital. The most complete service at any
hospital in the Unites States. Five hundred beds, splendid hotel, doctor's office
building, grill, barber shop, beauty shop, and one of the finest and most complete
drug stores in the Unites States – all under one roof with a garage adjoining."

[Pre 1920, $4-6]

GARTLY-RAMSAY HOSPITAL. INCORPORATED, MEMPHIS, TENN.

[Pre 1920, $4-6]

GARTLY-RAMSAY HOSPITAL, INCORPORATED, MEMPHIS, TENN.

GARTLY-RAMSAY HOSPITAL, INCORPORATED, MEMPHIS, TENN.

Gartly-Ramsay Hospital.
[pre 1920, $4-6]
696 Jackson Avenue.
Originally constructed in 1859 as a private
residence, the Gartly-Ramsay Hospital
opened in 1909 as a private care facility.
From 1950 to 1972 it housed a psychiatric hospital.
William Faulkner, perhaps the hospital's most famous
patient, was treated for alcohol addiction here.

Collins Chapel Correctional Hospital. [Linen era, $2-4]
416-418 Ashland Street.

Lynnhurst Sanitarium. [pre 1920, $4-6]
From the back: "Dr. S. T. Rucker's Private sanitarium for nervous diseases, mild mental disorders, and drug addictions. Beautiful park-like grounds. Elegance and comforts of well-appointed home.

The James Sanatorium. [pre 1915, $8-10]
Inscription: "The path to James Sanatorium, Raleigh Springs, Memphis, Tenn. which leads to good health, happiness, prosperity, and freedom from alcoholism, drug addictions, cigarette and tobacco habits. Illustrated and descriptive booklets containing testimonials, etc. mailed under plain cover. Address James Sanatorium, City Office 133 Poplar Ave., Memphis Tenn, U.S.A."

Tennessee Home for Incurables. [pre 1915, $6-8]
McLemore Ave.
From the back: "Just to be happy – 'tis a fine thing to do: To look on the bright side rather than the blue. Sad or sunny musing is largely to your choosing, And just being happy is brave work for you."

5362. W. O. W. Monument in Forest Hill Cemetery, Memphis, Tenn.

Woodmen of the World Monument in Forrest Hill Cemetery, Memphis, Tenn.

Woodmen of the World Monument. [pre 1915, $6-8]
Forest Hill Cemetery.

FOREST HILL CEMETERY, MEMPHIS.   113870

Forest Hill Cemetery. [pre 1920, $3-5]

W.O.W. Monument in Forest Hill Cemetery. [pre 1915, $6-8]

THE MAUSOLEUM, FOREST HILL CEMETERY, MEMPHIS. 113

The Mausoleum, Forest Hill Cemetery. [pre 1920, $3-5]
From the back: "The Modern Method of Burial. Space Available."

ENTRANCE TO ELMWOOD CEMETERY MEMPHIS. TENN.

SCENE IN ELMWOOD CEMETERY. MEMPHIS. TENN.

Elmwood Cemetery. [pre 1915, $4-6]

RECEIVING CHAPEL, FOREST HILL CEMETERY, MEMPHIS. 113876

Receiving Chapel, Forest Hill Cemetery. [pre 1920, $3-5]

Driveway, National Cemetery. [pre 1915, $2-4]

National Cemetery. [pre 1915, $4-6]

Confederate Monument in Elmwood Park. [pre 1915, $8-10]

10412. NATIONAL CEMETERY. MEMPHIS. TENN.

Driveway National Cemetery, Memphis, Tenn.

MEMPHIS, TENN. Confederate Monument. Elmwood Park.

CONFEDERATE DEAD.

NATIONAL CEMETERY ENTRANCE, MEMPHIS, TENN.

National Cemetery entrance. [pre 1915, $5-7]

Tell the World: "Special Care for Ladies and Children." ~ Phone 3-1068 and 3-2180

G. T. THOMAS

G. T. THOMAS FUNERAL HOME, 913 Mississippi Blvd., Memphis, Tenn.

The G.T. Thomas Funeral Home. [pre 1920, $10-12]
913 Mississippi Boulevard.

PHONE WAL. 82.   SPECIAL CARE FOR LADIES AND CHILDREN.

MRS. EMMA WILBURN WALTON FUNERAL HOME, 913 MISSISSIPPI BOULEVARD, MEMPHIS, TENN.

The Emma Wilburn Walton Funeral Home. [pre 1920, $6-8]
913 Mississippi Boulevard.
This card advertised "special care for ladies and children."

PHONE 3-0518—Local and Long Distance

FUNERAL HOME OF
T. H. HAYES & SONS

680 SO. LAUDERDALE ST.   MEMPHIS, TENN.

Funeral Home of T.H. Hayes and Sons. [pre 1920, $6-8]
680 S. Lauderdale St.
From the back: "The most modern in the South. The chapel with a
seating capacity of 200 is equipped with all modern equipment,
including a newly installed Pipe Organ of the latest and finest type. Our
personal attention is given to every call assuring the most sympathetic
and efficient service at all times with reasonable prices."

College Buildings & Schools

West Tennessee State Normal School Building. [pre 1920, $4-6]

WEST TENNESSEE STATE NORMAL SCHOOL BUILDING, NORMAL, TENN.

Library, State Teachers College, Memphis, Tenn.

Library, State Teachers College. [pre 1920, $4-6]

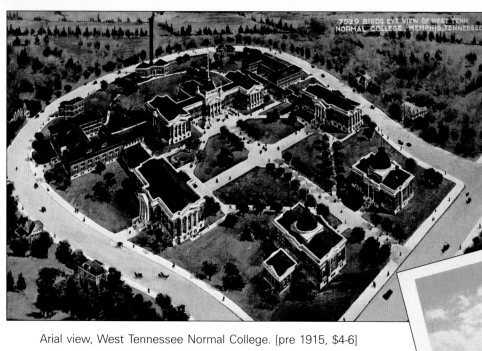

Arial view, West Tennessee Normal College. [pre 1915, $4-6]

Gymnasium and Boy's Dormitory, State Teachers College.
[pre 1920, $3-5]

Presidents House, State
Normal School. [pre 1920, $3-5]

Administration Building, State Teachers College. [pre 1920, $3-5]

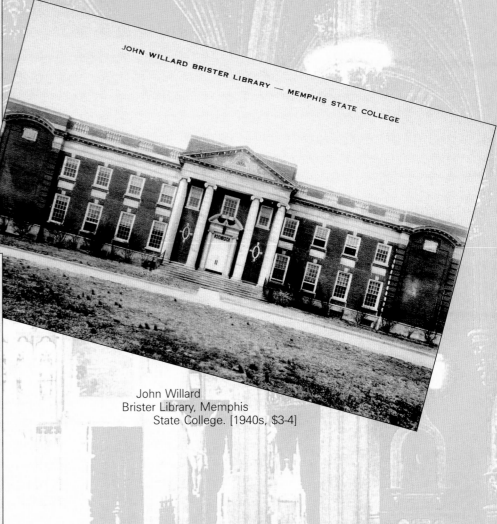

John Willard
Brister Library, Memphis
State College. [1940s, $3-4]

Main Building, West Tennessee State
Normal School. [pre 1920, $4-6]

ENTRANCE TO SOUTHWESTERN, "THE COLLEGE OF THE MISSISSIPPI VALLEY," MEMPHIS, TENN.—11

[pre 1920, $3-5]

SOUTHWESTERN, THE COLLEGE OF THE MISSISSIPPI VALLEY, MEMPHIS, TENN.   108751

Southwestern College. [pre 1920, $3-5]
Impressive stone pillars mark the entrance to "the College of the Mississippi Valley."
From the back: "Memphis' first college of liberal arts. Located on a beautiful wooded campus on North Parkway, opposite Overton Park, the buildings of vari-colored stone are among the finest examples of college architecture in the Unites States."

Multiple views of Southwestern University, the College of the Mississippi Valley. [Linen era, $2-4]

Southwestern University. [Linen era, $2-4]

Voorhies Hall, Southwestern College. [Linen era, $2-4]

PALMER HALL, SOUTHWESTERN COLLEGE, MEMPHIS, TENN.—65

Palmer Hall, Southwestern College. [Linen era, $2-4]

SOUTHWESTERN COLLEGE, MEMPHIS, TENNESSEE

The impressive architecture of Southwestern University. [Linen era, $2-4]

MEMPHIS UNIVERSITY SCHOOL
MEMPHIS, TENNESSEE C. 1900

FOUNDED BY E.S. WERTS AND J.W.S. RHEA IN 1893, THE ORIGINAL MEMPHIS UNIVERSITY SCHOOL MOVED FROM TEMPORARY QUARTERS TO THIS BUILDING IN 1899. ALTHOUGH THE OLD MUS CEASED OPERATIONS IN 1936, ITS IDEALS AND PRINCIPLES FURNISHED THE INSPIRATION FOR THE NEW MUS, FOUNDED AT PARK AND RIDGEWAY IN 1955.

Memphis University School. [1930s, $3-5]

St. Agnes Academy.
[pre 1915, $4-6]

5341. St. Agnes Academy, Memphis, Tenn.

Our New Home, Opposite the Famous Peabody Hotel, Main and Monroe
Write for Our Illustrated Catalogue

Macon-Andrews Business College, "Write for our
Illustrated Catalogue." [pre 1915, $5-7]
Main and Monroe St.

Interior Main Hall Macon & Andrews
Colleges. [pre 1915, $8-10]

INTERIOR MAIN HALL MACON & ANDREWS COLLEGES, MEMPHIS, TENN. U.S.A.

89

St. Mary's Academy. [pre 1920, $4-6]
253 N. Third.

High School building. [pre 1915, $4-6]

Central High School. [pre 1915, $4-6]

Stately manor homes along Waldron Avenue. [pre 1915, $4-6]

Fine residences. Stonewall
Place; Central Avenue; Peabody
Avenue. [pre 1915, $4-6]

Residence, Central Avenue. MEMPHIS, Tenn.

Tree-lined Central Avenue.
[pre 1915, $4-6]

Belvedere and Union Avenue. MEMPHIS, Tenn.

HISTORIC JAMES LEE HOME, MEMPHIS, TENN.

Historic James Lee Home. [pre 1920, $3-5]
Corner of Adams and N. Orleans St.
From the back: "This historic mansion is under a care and
restoration program of the Association for the preservation
of Tennessee Antiquities (A.P.T.A.). Located adjoining the
Fountaine House, it is one of the many attractions of historic
and period architecture of Memphis."

Belvedere and Union
Avenue. [pre 1915, $4-6]

Cultural Attractions & Recreation

From professional sports to casino gambling, Memphis continues to attract tourists from all over the world, offering a wide range of recreational activities. Music is a key entertainment attraction in Memphis, especially blues and rock and roll. Memphis also boasts two convention centers, the Pyramid, Peabody Place and Hotel, the Memphis Zoo and Aquarium, the Smithsonian Rock 'n' Soul Exhibit, Gibson Guitar Experience, the National Civil Rights Museum, The Pink Palace Museum, the McCarver Baseball Stadium, Fairgrounds, Mid-South Coliseum and Liberty Bowl, the Memphis Motorsports Park and the USA Rodeo Arena. Oh yes, and Graceland.

Parks

IN THE HEART OF MEMPHIS, TENN.—47

In the heart of Memphis. [pre 1920, $6-8] From the back: "The city has some of the finest parks and playgrounds in the country. The more than forty parks cover approximately 1,500 acres, all under the supervision of the Memphis Park Commission."

A GLIMPSE OF COURT SQUARE, MEMPHIS, TENN.

The band stand at Court Square. [pre 1915, $4-6]

Located in the heart of the Memphis business district, Court Square
is one of approximately forty parks in Memphis. [pre 1915, $4-6]

COURT SQUARE. MEMPHIS, TENN.

Court Square. [pre 1915, $8-10]

Japanese Garden, Overton Park. [pre 1920, $2-4]
From the back: "Like a corner of the Orient dropped down into the midst of the Occident, the Japanese Garden with its lily pond at Overton Park, is a vivid splotch of color. It is as fragrant as it is lovely. Children and grown-ups like to gather here to watch the water-fowl disport themselves."

Lily Pond in Forest Park. [pre 1920, $1-2]
From the back: "Lily pond in Overton Park [sic], one of the attractive spots in this spacious and beautiful park, which is one of the show places of the city. Memphis has 25 parks, with a total of 1155 acres."

7940. Pavilion in Overton Park, Memphis, Tenn.

Pavilion in Overton Park. [pre 1915, $4-6]
Overton Park, one of the largest urban parks in the country, is located in the heart of Midtown and is home to the Memphis Zoo, Memphis College of Art, Brooks Museum of Art, and the Overton Park Shell. It covers nearly 500 acres.

DOUGH BOY STATUE, OVERTON PARK, MEMPHIS, TENN.—30

Dough Boy Statue, Overton Park. [Linen era, $1-3]
From the back: "This statue, sponsored by the local Daughters of the American Revolution, was erected as a memorial to the World War dead of Memphis and Shelby County. It cost $15,000 raised by public subscription, to which Memphis school children contributed many thousands of pennies."

PAVILION AND PAGODA IN OVERTON PARK, MEMPHIS, TENN.—25

Pavilion and Pagoda in Overton Park. [Linen era, $1-2]
From the back: "Most beautiful of the thirty-two Memphis parks. Contains a nine-hole golf course, Doughboy Memorial Statue and Brooks Memorial Art Gallery."

96

BROOKS MEMORIAL ART GALLERY,
OVERTON PARK, MEMPHIS, TENN.—41

Brooks Memorial Art Gallery, Overton Park. [Linen era, $2-3]
From the back: "Here may be seen one of the finest collections of paintings and sculpture in the South. Loan collections from all over the world are on display at frequent intervals throughout the fall, winter, and spring months."

Brooks Memorial Art Gallery, Overton Park, Memphis Park Commission, City of Memphis. Tenn.

[pre 1920, $2-4]

Brooks Memorial Art
Gallery, Overton Park.
[Linen era, $1-2]
An impressive art gallery in the heart of Memphis, the
Brooks Memorial Art Gallery contains permanent collections of
Kress, the 18th and 19th century American, the International, the
Egyptian-Oriental, glass, porcelain, and lusterware collections.

BROOKS MEMORIAL ART GALLERY, OVERTON PARK, MEMPHIS, TENN.

[pre 1920, $2-4]

Riverside Park, Memphis. [pre 1920, $2-4]

From the back: "Memphis is noted for its beautiful parks and parkways. This "long, long trail awinding" takes the autoist [sic] amid the trees into a veritable honeymoon land, down the Riverside Park, where ever and anon one can catch a glimpse of the Mississippi River, on its journey to the Gulf of Mexico."

Drive in Riverside Park. [pre 1920, $1-3]

Riverside Park. [pre 1915, $2-3]

Higbee Memorial Monument, Memphis, Tenn.

GEN. FORREST MONUMENT IN FORREST PARK, MEMPHIS, TENN.——31

SUNKEN GARDEN AND ENTRANCE TO MORNINGSIDE PARK ON SPEEDWAY, MEMPHIS, TENN.

Higbee Memorial Monument. [pre 1920, $2-3]

General Forrest Monument in Forrest Park. [Linen era, $1-3] Bounded by Manassas and Dunlap Streets and Madison and Union Avenues.
Forrest Park honors the memory of General Nathan Bedford Forrest, Confederate hero of the Battle of Memphis. The monument is General Forrest's final resting place, as he lies buried beneath the statue.

Sunken Garden at Morningside Park on Speedway. [pre 1920, $2-3]

THE THIRD LARGEST ZOO IN THE UNITED STATES. MEMPHIS, TENN.

E-4165

Memphis Zoo. [Linen era, $2-4]
Billed as the third largest zoo in the United States, the Memphis Zoo was meticulously maintained and attracted visitors from all over.

ENTRANCE TO ZOO,
OVERTON PARK,
MEMPHIS, TENN.—55

Memphis Zoo, Overton Park. [Linen era, $1-3]
From the back: "Two lions, sculpted in Italy, adorn the entrance to the Memphis Zoological Garden. Brooks Memorial Art Gallery is also in Overton Park."

ENTRANCE TO MEMPHIS ZOO, MEMPHIS, TENNESSEE

Entrance to the Memphis Zoo. [Linen era, $1-3]

13398 THE BEAR PITS, MEMPHIS, TENN.   COPR. DETROIT PUBLISHING CO.

The Bear Pits, Memphis Zoo. [cancelled 1910, $8-10]
The back of the card advertised two points of interest
in Memphis: The Zoo and the Peabody Café.

CARNIVORA BUILDING, ZOO, OVERTON PARK, MEMPHIS, TENN.

The Carnivora Building, Overton
Park Zoo. [pre 1915, $5-6]

BEAR PIT AT ZOO, OVERTON PARK, MEMPHIS, TENN.

Bear Pit at the Zoo. [pre 1915, $6-8]

AL CHYMIA TEMPLE MEMPHIS BABY CAMEL 1910

BE NAMED FOR THE INCOMING IMPERIAL OUTER GUARD~NEW ORLEANS

Al Chymia Temple baby camel. [pre 1915, $8-10]

ELEPHANT HOUSE AT THE ZOO, OVERTON PARK, MEMPHIS, TENN.

Elephant House at the zoo,
Overton Park. [pre 1920, $6-8]

1580—THE FAMOUS AL CHYMIA SHRINE TEMPLE CAMEL. OVERTON PARK ZOO

The famous Al Chymia Shrine Temple camel. [pre 1920, $10-12]

Some of the animals that lived
and thrived at the Overton Park Zoo.
[pre 1915, $8-10]

Interior of Bird House, Overton Park Zoo, Memphis, Tenn.

Interior of the Bird House.
[pre 1920, $4-5]

Cub Leopard, Overton Park Zoo, Memphis, Tenn.

The Overton Park Zoo was considered one of the finest in the country. [Linen era, $5-6]

JAGUAR, MEMPHIS ZOO.   Pub. by Weaver Post Card Exchange, Memphis, Tenn.

The Memphis Zoo was quite well known for its varied animals. This card shows a jaguar. There were very few of these large animals in U.S. zoos at the time. [pre 1915, $6-8]

Reptile House, Overton Park Zoo, Memphis, Tenn.

Reptile House, Overton Park Zoo. [pre 1920, $3-5]

ENTRANCE, FAIRGROUNDS AMUSEMENT P

MEMPHIS FA

MEMPHIS, TENN.

ROUNDS

The entrance to the Memphis Fairgrounds
Amusement Park. [Linen era, $10-12]

THE GREAT TRI-STATE FAIR
AT MEMPHIS, TENN., SEPT. 28 TO OCT. 9, 1909

BIRDS-EYE VIEW OF TRI-STATE FAIR GROUNDS

COME AND MEET YOUR FRIENDS   THE BEST FAIR IN THE SOUTH

Birds-eye view of the Tri-State Fair,
September 28 to October 9, 1909.
[pre 1915, $10-12]

GIANT WHEELS, FAIRGROUNDS AMUSEMENT PARK, MEMPHIS, TENN.

Giant Wheels (Ferris Wheels), Fairgrounds
Amusement Park. [Linen era, $12-15]

THE WHIP, FAIRGROUNDS AMUSEMENT PARK, MEMPHIS, TENN.

Fairgrounds
Amusement
Park. "The
Whip." [Linen
era, $10-12]

108

THE PIPPIN, FAIRGROUNDS AMUSEMENT PARK, MEMPHIS, TENN.

Racing at the Tri State Fairgrounds. [cancelled 1911, $8-10]

"The Pippin" at the
Fairgrounds Amusement
Park. [Linen era, $12-15]

The Flamingo Room, Memphis' smartest night club. [1930s, $8-10] 140 1/2 Hernando St.

Lyceum Theatre. [cancelled 1907, $6-8]

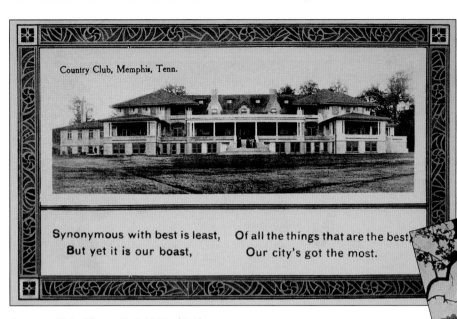

Country Club, Memphis, Tenn.

Synonymous with best is least,   Of all the things that are the best
   But yet it is our boast,   Our city's got the most.

Country Club. [Cancelled 1912, $6-8]
The verse: *Synonymous with best is least, But yet it is our boast,*
Of all the things that are the best, Our city's got the most.

7944. New Country Club, Memphis, Tenn.

Country Club - Golf Links, Memphis, Tenn.

Golf Links at
the Memphis Country
Club. [pre 1915, $8-10]

The New Country Club.
[pre 1915, $6-8]

111

Memphis Boat Club.
[pre 1915, $8-10]

Memphis, Tenn. Memphis Boat Club.

2522.

Hopkin's Grand Opera
House. [pre 1915, $8-10]

Memphis, Tenn. Hopkin's Grand Opera House.

2530.

Mississippi River Industry

The Mississippi River is key to the growth and development of Memphis, and indeed its very existence. The city first thrived as a river port and then a hub for rail transportation as well. The river served as the main route of transportation for people and goods into – and out of – Memphis. Cotton may have been king, but hardwood lumber was nearly as important; Memphis was one of the leading hardwood lumber markets in the world. Today, Memphis continues to be a major hub of goods and services, boasting thriving riverports as well as the busiest international cargo airport in the world.

Bridges

The Harahan Bridge, named for the president of the company that built it, was only the second railroad bridge to span the Mississippi River at Memphis. Completed in 1916, this huge construction project was responsible for the loss of at least twenty-three lives. From 1916 until 1949, cars navigated the river on two single-lane wooden-planked roadways precariously suspended on either side of the massive train trestle. These roadways were permanently closed in 1949.

There are many stories of strange happenings and events associated with the bridge. And no wonder. Eerily, Mr. J. T. Harahan, for whom the bridge was named, was killed when a train hit his car – four years before the completion of the project. During the decade of the Great Depression, some seventy desperate souls flung themselves off the bridge to a watery death, many of the bodies never recovered.

The connecting link between Tennessee on the east of the Mississippi River and Arkansas on the left. The river is approximately one-half mile wide at Memphis. [Linen era, $1-3]

THE CONNECTING L[

The three bridges which cross the Mississippi River at Memphis. The Frisco Bridge (right) was built in 1892, the Harahan Bridge (center) was completed in 1916, and the Tennessee-Arkansas Bridge, which was built in 1949 at a cost of over 16 million dollars. [Linen era, $1-3]

The Memphis and Harahan bridges, (before the Tennessee-Arkansas bridge was built) with U.S. Marine Hospital in the front. [Linen era, $2-4]

Memphis and Harrahan Bridges and U. S. Marine Hospital, Memphis, Tenn.   OB-H2126

HIS AND HARRAHAN BRIDGES SPANNING MISSISSIPPI RIVER, MEMPHIS, TENN.

THE SOUTH TO THE WEST—TENNESSEE ON THE EAST, ARKANSAS ON THE WEST

Spanning the Mississippi, the Memphis and Harahan Bridges. [Linen era, $2-4] From the back: "Two railway bridges cross the Mississippi River at Memphis, the only bridges south of the Ohio. One of them, the Harahan Bridge, provides vehicular traffic. Five of the eight national highways, routed through Memphis, cross the river on this bridge."

Memphis and Harahan Bridges Spanning Mississippi River, Memphis, Tenn.—1

MEMPHIS AND HARRAHAN BRIDGES. MEMPHIS. TENN.

GATEWAY TO THE WEST JOINING ARKANSAS AND TENNESSEE

Memphis and Harahan Bridges. [Linen era, $2-4] Gateway to the west joining Arkansas and Tennessee.

Harahan Bridge. [Linen era, $2-4]

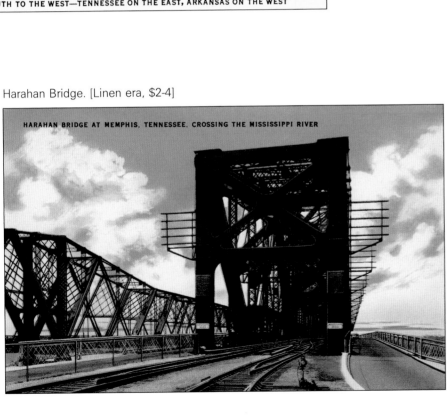

HARAHAN BRIDGE AT MEMPHIS, TENNESSEE, CROSSING THE MISSISSIPPI RIVER

SKY-LINE AND RIVER FRONT, MEMPHIS, TENN.

Memphis skyline and river front. [Linen era, $4-6]

13402 SKYLINE FROM THE RIVER, MEMPHIS, TENN.

View of the Memphis skyline, taken from
the Mississippi River. [pre 1920, $4-6]

Waterfront, Memphis, Tenn.—20

Copyright 1923 Bluff City Engraving Co., Memphis.

Waterfront. [pre 1920, $3-5]
From the back: "Memphis, Tenn., Down in
Dixie, the financial, industrial, commercial and
social capital of the lower Mississippi Valley, is
the greatest inland cotton market in the world,
the world's largest hardwood lumber produc-
ing market and the great distribution center of
the middle South, located on the east bank of
the Mississippi River, about midway between
the Great Lakes and the Gulf of Mexico."

Memphis from Miss. River, Memphis, Tenn.

Advertising card – Memphis from the Mississippi River, compliments of A.W. Robinson and Co. Lumber. [cancelled 1908, $6-8]

Approaching Memphis.

COMPLIMENTS OF
B. R. WELLFORD
1003 TENN. TRUST BLDG.
ACCIDENT INSURANCE
FIRE INSURANCE
REAL ESTATE

Approaching Memphis. [cancelled 1906, $6-8]

7952. Harbor and Water Front, Memphis, Tenn.

Memphis Harbor and Water Front. [cancelled 1915, $6-8]

117

Race between the
Natchez and the Robert E. Lee.
[pre 1920, $4-6]

Steamer J.S. De Luxe on the Mississippi River. [Linen era, $2-4]
From the back: "The Steamer travels the entire Mississippi from New Orleans to St. Paul and the Ohio river from Cairo to Pittsburgh."

The famous Steamboat "Robert E. Lee," loading cotton, Mississippi River Landing. [Linen era, $2-4] The time made by the R.E. Lee from New Orleans to St. Louis in 1870 in her famous race with the Natchez, is the best on record. The R.E. Lee arrived ahead of the Natchez by six hours and fourteen minutes.

U.S. Gunboat on Mississippi River. [pre 1915, $6-8]

Steamer, the Stacker
Lee. [cancelled 1908, $6-8]

Mississippi River boat, the "James Lee." [cancelled 1908, $6-8]

Freight barges on the river, approaching Memphis. [Linen era, $2-3]

The Memphis riverfront. [pre 1915, $6-8]

Scenes such as this were common along the Mississippi, particularly at Memphis, a leading shipping port on the River. [pre 1915, $8-10]

At the Wharf. [pre 1915, $8-10]

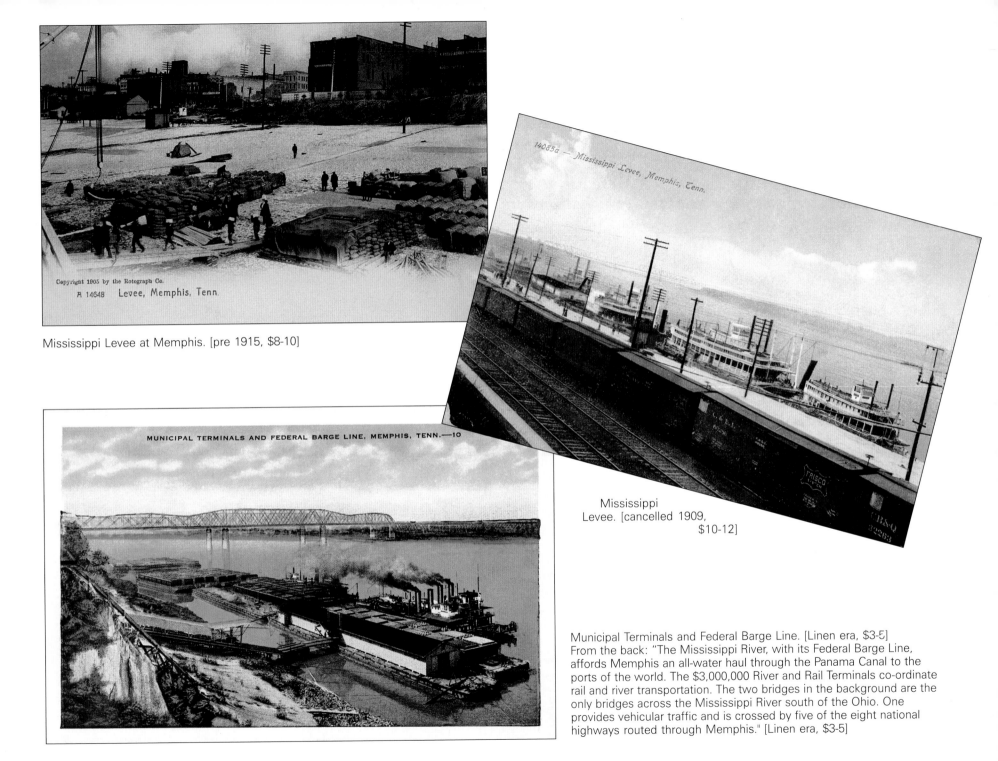

Copyright 1905 by the Rotograph Co.
A 14648   Levee, Memphis, Tenn.

Mississippi Levee at Memphis. [pre 1915, $8-10]

14085a — Mississippi Levee, Memphis, Tenn.

Mississippi
Levee. [cancelled 1909,
$10-12]

MUNICIPAL TERMINALS AND FEDERAL BARGE LINE, MEMPHIS, TENN.—10

Municipal Terminals and Federal Barge Line. [Linen era, $3-5]
From the back: "The Mississippi River, with its Federal Barge Line,
affords Memphis an all-water haul through the Panama Canal to the
ports of the world. The $3,000,000 River and Rail Terminals co-ordinate
rail and river transportation. The two bridges in the background are the
only bridges across the Mississippi River south of the Ohio. One
provides vehicular traffic and is crossed by five of the eight national
highways routed through Memphis." [Linen era, $3-5]

Cotton

In the Cotton Fields. [pre 1915, $8-10]

Cotton and lumber, the two main products for which Memphis is known, were shipped in huge quantities from its many ports. [pre 1920, $8-10]

Memphis was known as the "city of white gold" for the high quality cotton that shipped from its ports. [Linen era, $4-6]

Cotton ginning time in Memphis. [Linen era, $4-6]

Early view
of a cotton gin.
[Cancelled 1911, $15-20]

"A mountain of cotton
seeds." [cancelled
1911, $15-20]

This postcard, posted in 1910, shows the *Katie Robbins* laden with cotton shipping from the waterfront in Memphis. [pre 1915, $8-10]

Boat loaded with Cotton, Memphis, Tenn.

THE LEVEE FROM THE BLUFF, MEMPHIS, TENN.

A view of the Levee, looking down from the bluff. [pre 1920, $3-5]

124

Lumber

Loading logs on a tram car.
[pre 1915, $8-10]

ONE OF THE MANY LUMBER MILLS AND YARDS AT MEMPHIS. TENN.

One of the many lumber mills and lumber yards in Memphis. [Linen era, $4-6]
From the back: "Memphis is the largest inland hardwood lumber market in the world. Three hundred million feet of hardwood lumber are turned out of here, annually, valued at $52,000,000.00. Local mills turn out doors, blinds, sashes, screens, as well as lumber for every conceivable purpose. Furniture and auto body parts are also manufactured here."

Levee, showing the principal products shipped from Memphis, cotton and hardwood. [pre 1915, $8-10]

Shipment of logs on the Mississippi River. [pre 1915, $8-10]

A Short History of the Postcard in the United States

Pioneer Era (1893-1898)

Although there were earlier scattered issues, most pioneer cards in today's collections begin with the cards placed on sale at the Columbian Exposition in Chicago, Illinois, on May 1, 1893. These were illustrations on government printed postal cards and privately printed souvenir cards. The government postal cards had the printed one-cent stamp, while the souvenir cards required a two-cent adhesive postage stamp to be applied. Writing was not permitted on the address side of the cards.

Private Mailing Card Era (1898-1901)

On May 19, 1898, private printers were granted permission, by an act of Congress, to print and sell cards that bore the inscription "Private Mailing Card." Today, they are called "PMCs." A one-cent adhesive stamp was required. A dozen or more American printers began to take postcards seriously. Writing was still not permitted on the address side.

Postcard Era (1901-1907)

The use of the word "Postcard" was granted by the government to private printers on December 24, 1901. Writing was still not permitted on the address side. In this era, private citizens began to take black-and-white photographs and have them printed on paper with postcard backs.

Divided Back Era (1907-1914)

Postcards with a divided back were permitted March 1, 1907. The address was to be written on the right side and the left side was for writing messages. Many millions of cards were published and printed in this era, most in Germany, where printers were far more advanced in the lithographic processes. With the advent of World War I, the supply of postcards had to come from England and the United States.

White Border Era (1915-1930)

Most domestic-use postcards were printed in the United States during this period. To save ink, a border was left around the view, thus the name "White Border Cards." The high cost of labor, inexperience, and public taste created cards of inferior quality. Competition in a narrowing market caused many publishers to go out of business.

Linen Era (1930-1944)

New printing processes allowed printing on postcards with high rag content that caused a linen-like finish. These cheap cards allowed for the use of gaudy dyes for coloring. Curt Teich's line of linen postcards flourished. Many important historical events are recorded on these cards.

Bibliography

Bond, Beverly G. and Janann Sherman. *Memphis: In Black and White*. Charleston, South Carolina: Arcadia, 2003.

Dawson, David B. *Memphis: New Visions, New Horizons (Urban Tapestry Series)*. Towery Publishing, 1997.

Emporis, http://www.emporis.com/en/wm/ci/bu/?id=101918, (21 January 2005).

Goodspeed *s History of Hamilton, Knox and Shelby Counties of Tennessee* Publisher: Elders Bookstore, 1974. http://www.wdbj.net/shelby/goodspeed/history/index.html (19 January 2005).

Harkins, John. *Metropolis of the American Nile: A History of Memphis & Shelby County, Tennessee*. Oxford, Mississippi: Guild Bindery Press, 1995.

Insiders' Guide to Memphis: Guilford, Connecticut: Globe Pequot Press, 2002.

Johnson, Judith, "The Art of Architecture: Modernism In Memphis 1890 – 1980, http://www.memphisheritage.org/MHIHost/Read-ModernismInMemphis.html, 16 February, 2005).

Memphis Heritage, Historic Properties list. http://www.memphisheritage.org/MHIHost/INDEX.html, (28 March 2005).

Memphis Magazine, http://www.memphismagazine.com, January 11, 2005).

Shelby County Tennessee Genealogy and History, http://www.wdbj.net/shelby/index.html

Soul of America, Churches/Historic sites list. http://www.soulofamerica.com/cityfldr/memphis4.html (10 February 2005).

Index of Major Buildings